LIGHTHOUSE

Lakeya Brown

Lighthouse Copyright © 2017 Lakeya Brown

ISBN: 978-1-7349101-1-7

All rights reserved. No part of this publication may be reproduced, distributed, or transmitted in any form without the prior written permission of the author, except in the case of brief quotations embodied in reviews and certain other noncommercial uses permitted by copyright law.

Contents

Dear Readers, ... 10

The Space Between 12

Lessons Learned 13

Life Storms 14

Falling is the Gift 15

Keeping Watch 16

Authenticity 18

To My Younger Self 19

Rock of Ages 20

Made To Withstand 21

She 22

Keep Going 23

There Will Come a Time 24

Anger 25

Do Not Fear 26

Valleys and Mountains 27

This Hurts 28

Fully Known 29

Anchored 30

When They Ask 31

New Day 32

Why 33

When The Storm Passed 34

Careful 36

Just a Friendly Reminder	37
When My Foot Slips	38
No Matter	39
Hardest Thing	40
Let it Be	41
Swallowed	42
Doors	43
Growth	44
I Choose	45
Stabbed	46
Before	47
Get Out of the Boat	48
Every Day	49
Feeling the Vulnerability	51
Kindled	52
Envy	53
It's Not You	54
Keepin' it Real	55
Flaws	56
Falling Into Place	57
I Watched	58
Choosing	60
Stayed Too Long	61
Safe Place	62
Until	63

Blanket of Lies 64

Words..65

The Process 66

Cherishing the Breath 67

True Friendship..68

Real 69

Sister to Sister...70

When Your Storm Comes 71

Sometimes...72

Missing...73

Inhale Courage, Exhale Doubt.......................74

Inevitability of Brokenness 75

What a Shame 76

Wild and Free...77

Bare 78

Extra Pieces 79

What is For Me 80

Lies We Tell 81

Decision 82

Heart Failure...83

People Want to Know Me 84

Unsure..85

Forgery 86

I Knew It Was You...87

I Felt You 88

Root Down and Grow 89

I Know 91

Feed You 92

Light 93

Sometimes 94

Moving Forward 95

Imperfections Only 96

Exposed 97

Beautiful Places 98

Darkness You Don't Scare Me 99

Be Strong Be courageous 100

Storms 101

Closer, Cleaner, Relief 102

Unpack 103

Man-Made Storms 104

Rhythm 105

Exit Wounds 106

A Warriors Scar 107

Feel It 108

One After Another 109

Two-way Mirror 110

Joy 112

Blue Balloon 113

Keep Moving 114

Tap Out 115

Lost 116
Each Step Back 117
Nothing Left Behind 118
Relax 119
Scrapes 120
Leave it Alone 121
Boundaries 122
I Heard You 123
Lost Yourself 124
Direction 125
Undeniable Earth 126
Thunderstorms 127
Pen and Paper 128
Not a Threat 129
Strong 130
Living on Purpose 131
Your Soul Deserves 132
My Tears 133
A Story For All 134
First Save Yourself 135
Just Like That 136
When to Begin 137
You Created Me 138
If You Do 139
Shining 140

The Act of Forgiveness 141

Simply Wait 142

Empathy and Love 143

Safe to Rest 144

Walking Along the Shore 145

The Sun 146

Breathe 147

What We Fear 148

I Miss the Innocence of It All 150

How to Measure Relationships 151

But First 152

You Must Believe 153

Every Mistake 154

Save Yourself 156

You Had a Choice 158

Feed the Universe 159

Thrive 160

Don't Listen 161

That Night 162

No Regrets 163

If It Must Be 164

When the pain was too much to bear, I closed my tear-stained eyes and whispered, help me, God. Help me and when you have lifted the pain and healed my brokenness, I will help you lead others out of the darkness.

-For the light bearers and those lost at sea

LIGHTHOUSE

Dear Readers,

I hope my collection of poems soothes the sore from the constant beatings of life. I hope it encourages you to look ahead, and keep moving past the debris that life's storms keep throwing at you. Don't get stuck in the hurt, the pain and the shames of life. Immerse yourself in the pain. Feel it deeply and then begin to heal. Some pains, you will have to let them heal on their own. Remove your hands from it and stop irritating it. And for other pains you will have to put foot to action and show up for yourself.

We are all lighthouses, bearers of the light that shines from within. Learn your lessons, grow, clean your wounds and begin to heal. Don't waste your life by allowing bitterness from harsh lessons to consume you. Your journey is not just about you. Others need our stories, our hearts, our healing balms, and our lights. There are so many lost at sea, searching for the guide that only a lighthouse, a light bearer can offer. Humble yourself, let compassion and empathy consume you.

We may never understand the reasons for some of our storms. It is alright. Release the need to know why. Understand that no matter how dark it may seem the rain will eventually stop.

Know that there is a lesson to be learned, and a blessing to be added to your life.

LIGHTHOUSE

The Space Between

The space between where you are
and where you want to be,
is where life's storms occur.
Not to discourage you, but to inspire
you to move into the depth and the greatness
stored within you.

LAKEYA BROWN

Lessons Learned

You keep wishing them away,
but it won't go away.
It is here to teach you some things.
Things you will need for the rest
of your journey.

It is here to unlock your
extraordinary potential.
It breaks you of your stubbornness
and forces you to the path of your purpose.
You see, you can't wish it away
or pray it away.
It's here to stay until you learn from it.

Life Storms

The pain, the rain, and the darkness
of the storm.
It is all for you to learn that you are indeed a
powerful bearer of the light.
You were created not for your purpose, but to
help others pull through the storm by learning
through your life storms.

Every time you learn a lesson, your light shines
brighter to guide others lost at sea safely to
shore, safely home.
Never stop learning, and never stop embracing
your mistakes.
You are the lighthouse,
which houses the beacon of light.

Falling is the Gift

When you take your hands away
and allow people to fall, it is a gift.
A gift in the form of a lesson.
They get to hit the ground.
They experience the miracle of
brokenness, bruising, scarring,
and the enchantment of healing.
They get to choose what happens next.

LIGHTHOUSE

Keeping Watch

I stand upon the rock securely cemented.
Confidently and awesomely made.
I stand.
Taking in the flood, withstanding impact
after impact, bracing for each crashing wave.

Angels protect me.
Rocks reinforce me, waves drench me,
then return to the sea.
I remain.
I am safe upon the rock as
the chaos encamps me.

My light shines fiercely from within,
to call home all who are lost at sea.
Humbled by the light that shines from within.
Grateful for the nights that formed me,
and thankful for the lessons that chose me.

LAKEYA BROWN

Foundation

When you build too fast the foundation
never really settles.
It cracks and begins to run like
a new pair of pantyhose.

So, when you build, let the foundation settle.
Wait for it to become complete.
Otherwise, the storm will come and wash
it all away and you will have used all of your
resources and have nothing to show for it.

Authenticity

It is my authenticity that sets
me apart and draws them in.
Like a magnet, my light
calls out to their light within.

LAKEYA BROWN

To My Younger Self

To my younger self,
be to yourself who you need in that moment.
To my adult self,
let go and be who you need in this moment.
To my younger self,
you need these lessons, so pay attention.
To my older self,
remain calm and recall each lesson.

Rock of Ages

Calm seas, calm winds, pulling the water out,
then in towards me.
Never really learning, never really growing,
just going with the flow.
But going with the flow was never intended
to be my story.

So, I wasn't surprised when the internal winds
began to roar.
Friction and tension blending with the
troubled and calm air,
creating the perfect storm.
It wasn't until the waters of my life
viscously surrounded me.

It wasn't until I crashed against the rock of
ages, that the chaos erupted, and his love and
peace flowed into me.

Made To Withstand

A lighthouse is strong.
It does not worry about the rain.
It knows that it was built to withstand
the deadliest of storms.
Day and night, night and day,
it humbly stands.

It is confident.
Knowing that it houses a powerful
beacon of light.
Shining it's light and encroaching
into every dangerous, dark spots,
and guiding ships while out at sea.
It knows defeat could never prosper.
So it withstands storm after storm,
tsunami and earthquake.

LIGHTHOUSE

She

In the places that are hidden, she weeps.
Afraid to let go, and afraid to step forward.
So, she stays behind the filth.
She stands in the dark corners
hidden, and weeping within.

Afraid to change because
who will she be without the pain?
Who will she be without the
agony, resentment, anger,
or the impenetrable wall?

What will protect her?
Who will keep her safe?
How will she operate in this change?

She is you.
She is me.
She is us.
She is the little girl within,
afraid to grow into
the Princess,
the Queen,
the Woman,
destined to be.

Keep Going

I know it's hard, but keep going.
Keep moving.
Keep putting one foot in front of the other.
Don't look down.
Don't look back.
Just fix your eyes ahead,
taking it second by second,
Minute by minute.
Breathe.
Keep going, keep moving.

LIGHTHOUSE

There Will Come a Time

There will come a time when the
storm will cease its violence and the
clouds will have cried their final tear.

You will remember each storm,
and trace your fingers along the scars,
but you will no longer feel that agonizing pain.

Instead, you will feel a slight sensation and
know that something dark and strong once
lived in the walls of those scars.

When you look over those scars you will
remember that you are nothing like you use to
be and you could never go back to where you
were.

Anger

It stirs.
The cool breeze mixes with the warm breeze.
It stirs not swiftly, but patiently taking form.

The air suffocates you.
It takes over and refuses to let you go.
It rages, becoming violent,
and uncontrollably dangerous.

Faulty storm drains work overtime,
rapidly filling high.
Wreckage wildly flies, blocking all exits.
This must be what it feels like to
drown from the inside out.

Do Not Fear

Don't be afraid.
You're going to break,
you're going to fall apart,
but you will pick yourself up,
you will heal.
Not all at once,
but piece by piece,
fiber by fiber.
And this time you'll
be better than before.

LAKEYA BROWN

Valleys and Mountains

There are moments when you will feel
level to the ground.
When you have climbed to the mountain top
only to be kicked back down into the valley.
There are moments when you feel like you
just may plummet to what feels like your
demise.

When you will have to crawl
more than you will walk.
You will appear to be smaller
than you really are.
Embrace it.
Embrace these difficult moments.
There is a treasure within you.

You are not alone.
You are right where you are supposed to be,
at this moment.
You are not forsaken.
You can only train in the valley.
You can only win victories in the trenches.

This Hurts

When you have to let the pain inside, it hurts.
You will have to let the pain rise to its
peak and clean the unhealed wounds.
When you have to let it pus, scab,
and scar, it hurts.

Drenched eyes flood your soul.
Sobs and strained breaths through hard
pressed hearts and a grieved spirit will occur.
Let the process happen,
your spirit knows what to do.

Let it hurt.
Don't numb the pain.
It is necessary to heal.

Fully Known

Storms allow your fearful heart to
curl its back against understanding.
If you allow it, the storm teaches
you that you are deeply loved
and fully known.

Anchored

I've learned that it is not my
job to be anyone's anchor.
I have abandoned myself.
While trying to anchor others
I've drowned repeatedly,
without realizing that I was
not securely anchored.

When They Ask

When they ask you if you are alright,
it's okay to say NO.
I repeat, when they ask if you are okay,
and you are not,
it is alright to say an honest NO.
You are under no obligation to say yes.

It is alright to say that today the grey clouds
have rolled in and I was hoping for clear skies.
It is alright to tell them that you feel like a
deflated balloon.

That you feel like a bird with broken wings.
It won't always be grey skies,
deflated balloons can be replaced and broken
wings can heal when treated correctly.
You can say NO.
I give you permission.

New Day

Every day is a new day.
Just know, if you didn't
get it right yesterday,
today offers a clean slate.
Use it wisely.

LAKEYA BROWN

Why

When I close my eyes,
the night does not quickly pass by.
You said, weeping may endure for a night,
but the x's on my calendar reads night 101,934
and I'm still waiting
for the joy in the morning.
Rocking myself to sleep each night,
repeatedly asking why.

Then one night as I slept, I heard a gentle
voice say, I have come to teach you not to fear
the dark, to help you shine and master
the art of letting go.

You see letting go is essential to your peace.
I sent the storm each time stronger and
stronger, but you won't let go of that
which weighs you down.
My dear, this is the answer to your why.

LIGHTHOUSE

When The Storm Passed

When the storm has passed by,
I knew you were the only shelter
in times of the storm.
I knew that your love was greater
than any unkind wave.
I now understand that when I go
through deep waters you will be with me.
That as I reach up you will reach down
to draw me out if ever I should fall overboard.

LAKEYA BROWN

Trust Exercise

He asked me to trust him.
Put my arms out and fall back into the security
and peace that was his arms.

My stomach churned agreeing with the
conflicting thoughts flooding my head.
Trust him, let go and trust him
one thought at a time.

Are you crazy?
He will drop you like all the others before him,
and this time there will be no
putting the pieces back together.

"Trust me," his voice said, cutting
through my surmounting thoughts.
"I'm not strong enough,
I'm not courageous enough,"
I rebutted almost to tears.

"I'll show you strong, I'll show you
courageous, I'll show you faith in action
just trust me," he said.

"When you're ready to fall into my arms you'll
see that I am ready to catch you,
I've always been ready to catch you".

LIGHTHOUSE

Careful

Even when you are cruel to yourself
God is kind to you.
He waits patiently for you to see what
He sees in you.
Even when you push him away,
God is careful with you
until you learn to be careful with yourself.

LAKEYA BROWN

Just a Friendly Reminder

Just a friendly reminder
that you are beautiful,
you are complete,
you are strong.
No matter what it looks like,
you are enough.

When My Foot Slips

Sometimes I feel my foot slipping
and my knees buckle beneath me.
It scares me.
Then I remember that God is within
me and he won't let me fall.

LAKEYA BROWN

No Matter

No matter how violent the storm
or dark the night may be,
if the direction in which you are
Sailing towards is unhealthy, unsafe,
and unpurposeful,
you don't have to wait until the
morning to turn your ship around
and sail into better territories.

LIGHTHOUSE

Hardest Thing

The hardest thing to do in this life,
is to keep going when it looks like
nothing is changing.

Let it Be

Sometimes you want to
cover up the wounds.
Hide them, fix them.
Don't!
Let it remain exposed,
let it be.

Swallowed

People see you lose many battles.
They laugh and mock, saying the
storm swallowed you whole.
They will say that it must have
been your fault, you had to have
done something wrong.

Naturally, they will acknowledge
the defeat, but never acknowledge
that the storms, and the battles
cleaned you up and made you better.

They will ignore that the storm
swallowed you whole, but spat
you out, ensuring you landed
on your feet.

Doors

The door was shut,
but you said you needed closure.
Reopening what had been
bolted for you own protection.
You let the toxic, cold, and dark back in.
The darkness refuses,
it has nonself-control, and no morals.
It forces your heart open, and violates you.
Leaving its seeds, a million give or take
surviving in your walls, buried in your home.
The locks were changed and now it's darkness's
home, because when it rang the doorbell you
chose to open the door.
Now you're a squatter in your own home.

Growth

Growth hurts.
It is one of the most uncomfortable
things you will ever experience.
It drags you into unfamiliar
and unsafe territories.
Sometimes the pain and agony become marred
with feelings of hopelessness
and may feel unbearable.
Accept the challenge of growth
and stop fighting it.
It has been sent to make sure your process is
completed.
For each lesson,
growth forces you to become.
Regret nothing and grow through everything.

I Choose

I choose life, I choose love.
I choose happiness, I choose peace.
I choose to no longer be placed in a box,
or curl my aching back against the comfort of mediocrity.
I choose to no longer live in fear.
Stunting my growth because I am too afraid of failing.
I choose to no longer dim my light because others think it too bright.

Stabbed

The flesh you took when you stabbed me in
my back, that doubled around to my heart
is yours to keep.
You'll look for me in others,
but never find me.
Consider it a parting gift.
Cherish it as you would a souvenir.
Remember it as you roam the seas,
climb the mountains and probe the valleys.
Remember it as you frantically lose yourself in
others, all the while searching for pieces of the
beauty, which can only be found within me.

Before

Before you love anyone else
make sure you love yourself.
Before you have another's back,
make sure you have your own.
Before you forgive anyone else,
make sure you have forgiven yourself.
Before you pray for anyone else,
make sure you pray for yourself.
Before you judge anyone else's fruit,
make sure you inspect and judged your fruit.
Make sure that the standards you measure
against are not the fickle standards of society.
Make sure they are God's and yours alone.

Get Out of the Boat

When the storms are raging
Jesus bids you to come and
walk on water.
So don't judge those sinking.
You don't understand the weight they carry,
nor the faith it took to step out of that boat
into the water.
You see them drowning but
God sees them trying.

LAKEYA BROWN

Every Day

Every day you live this life you run the risk of
being stretched, or wounded
and permanently scarred.
Ask yourself honestly, how much of this pain
is caused by your actions
and selfish ambitions.

Remain honest.
How much of this pain remains because
you choose not to let go of what hurts
you the most?
Let go and give yourself the gift
and grace to heal.

LIGHTHOUSE

Burning Bridges

I was told to never burn my bridges.
So as painful, damaged, and dangerous
as they were, I kept them.
With each crossing, I lost a piece of myself.
Each time drifting farther,
and farther away from my truth.

I know you said not to burn any bridges
because I might have to cross over again,
but this bridge is killing me.
This bridge is destroying me
and slowly draining the soul out of me.

So turn away, because this time when I cross, it will be different.
This time I will stand in the middle,
making sure it is drenched in gasoline.
There will be no bridge to salvage,
no bridge to cross, from your side or mine.

Feeling the Vulnerability

It's alright to be vulnerable,
to be sensitive, and to be weak.
We deceive ourselves by saying
we are invincible and untouchable.
Amazing, strong, intelligent,
and powerful creations we are.

Yet it is alright to be exposed,
delicate, and frail.
It celebrates our humanity
and testifies of our complexities.

It shouts throughout the earth
and echoes throughout the heavens,
that you are strong enough to
be weak enough to be strong.

LIGHTHOUSE

Kindled

My fire had begun to burn out.
I was searching frantically for light.
Searches became obsessions
and obsessions became fixation that
would burn bright for a while,
then slowly burn out.

I've never burned brighter than the day
I stepped out of myself and into your
all-consuming fire.
You are the fire that I've searched for
my whole life.

Envy

People will see the aftermath,
your rebuilding after the storm.
They will come from near
and far to see the beauty of your rebuilding.

They will take credit saying,
"I supplied a brick",
"I gave the straws",
"I supplied the light",
"I provided cheap labor".

They will envy and even boil
over with jealousy, at the sight
of your newness.
So you will have to be bold
and say, "don't envy my arrival
unless you've envied my struggle".

It's Not You

It's not you, it's them.
When you are solid, when
you are secure, it scares people.
They are afraid to break,
to step out of the shallow and
risk drowning in your depth.

Keepin' it Real

I tried to keep it real, but you
abused me with your silence.
I tried to keep it real, but you
called my feelings garbage.

I can't be real here so I will not
unpack here.
I will not stay here.
I choose to keep it moving.

Moving to a place where my truth
can exist at-large.
A place where I can let my anchor
down and dock for a while.

Flaws

When you fall in love with your flaws,
and make peace with your insecurities,
no one would ever gain control over you.
No one would ever use them as a weapon
to destroy you.

Falling Into Place

The things that we believe
are falling apart,
are actually falling
into their predestined places.

So I no longer try
to hold myself together,
I welcome the experience
of beautifully falling apart.

LIGHTHOUSE

I Watched

I watched as a feather detached
and flew apart from a bird once.
Intrigued, mesmerized,
and somehow envious.

I couldn't decide if I wanted
to be the bird or the feather.
The feather flew for a while
as I walked below it.

It flew for miles, landing and
beautifully plié-ing
tree to tree, then floating
again on air.

I knew separated from the bird
it had no purpose,
but I was jealous of how free
that feather looked.

Dancing from tree to tree,
landing in such beautiful form.
It landed on the ground
and scurried around for a bit.

I stooped and waited for it to
fly again, but it didn't.
So I picked it up and blew it
up towards the sky.

At that moment I knew
I wanted to be the bird.
Taking off and always landing
with a purpose.

Choosing

When it comes to choosing.
I will
ALWAYS
Choose me.

Stayed Too Long

I stayed in this relationship for too long.
Devalued, diminished, demeaned,
and broken.
I called it loyalty,
you called it a relationship.
We named it friendship,
but the red flags labeled it foolish.
Now, I label it me breaking my own heart.

Safe Place

When you have found your safe place
physically,
when you have found your safe place
emotionally,
when you have found your safe place mentally,
when you have found your safe place
spiritually,
you become a light for others
to find their safe place.

Until

Until you really find out who you are,
and what you have been created to do.
Until you come to the end of yourself,
you will continue to crack, fumble,
and break those who try to get close to you.
That is what you do when you're hurting.

You inflict pain on everyone else around
you and label it love.
You minimize your dysfunction and shrug
it off by rationalizing and thinking, they
just weren't strong enough to love me.
But really, you weren't strong enough
to love yourself.

Blanket of Lies

Some people want to live in truth,
but they can't.
They are afraid of what the truth will expose.
So they carry lies around like Linus
and his blanket.
It doesn't matter if it is tattered,
or torn with holes the sized of cannon balls.
They will carry it because it is their warmth,
it is their security.

It serves them purpose.
Some people want to live in truth,
but they won't.
So they tell themselves they can't.
But if they shall ever discard of the blanket,
they will see that the warmth from the truth
can be more freeing
and satisfying than any lie.

Words

Words.
They get stuck in your hair.
When spoken, they stick to your skin
and sip into the layers of you.
They enter your blood stream
and become lodged in the walls of your heart.

Those words become your core beliefs.
The story of who you are,
where you come from,
and where you are going.
Make sure the words that are spoken
are your own healthy words.
Be sure to guard your heart.

The Process

When you are complete and whole,
you tend to forget that at one point
you were not.
You forget that you were once broken, hurting,
foul, and merciless.
That you had to mourn the loss of the fairy-
tale, the false-expectations, the what-if,
should-have, and would-have been.

Let people go through their process.
Forgive them because they may be hurting.
Forgive them in their incomplete stage.
Correct them with love, while giving them
the space to complete the process of healing.

LAKEYA BROWN

Cherishing the Breath

First, it washes over you, a lot.
Wave after wave.
No time for deep breaths,
only shallow breaths.

The earth and the moon play tug-a-war
as you fight for breaths.
Then little by little the waves resend
allowing you draw deeper breaths
than ever before.

True Friendship

Pay attention to the friend who dances with
you in the rain.
They aren't afraid of the wet caused
by ladened clouds.

If they will walk with you in scattered
showers, they will walk with you during
roaring thunder, flashing lightening,
and life-threatening storms.

There is no need to feel alone,
they're here to stay.
Never afraid to walk unsheltered,
to the places they are granted access to
during your storm.

Real

I no longer search for the good in others
I search for the real in them instead.
Good sets itself apart in the most elegant
of clothing, while real proudly says,
"Here I am, naked and unashamed".

LIGHTHOUSE

Sister to Sister

If you forget my face,
if I lose my voice,
remember this if nothing else.
Remember that wherever you go
I. Love. You.
Whatever you do, I'm proud of you.

Remember, no matter the obstacle,
I will always be here for you
without compulsion, but with much
conviction and abundant love.
Know that I will forever stand in the
darkness, sit in the shade, walk in the
sunshine, and lay under the blushing,
star-kissed night sky.

LAKEYA BROWN

When Your Storm Comes

When your storms come just know that
you are not alone.
Know that I will not speak
because that is not what you need.

I will sit here knowing I could be
swallowed up by the floods.
I will wait in the madness of your storm.

When the thunderous voice of your chaos
screams for me to move, and uproot
unstable trees, I will remain here.

I will be unmovable.
I will sit quietly, shielding you
with the umbrella of my prayers
until the storm passes.

Sometimes

Sometimes you just have to look in the
mirror and say, don't cry pretty girl.
Cheer up!
Be bold, stand tall, and be courageous.

It's supposed to hurt sometimes,
It's supposed to sting sometimes,
It's supposed to be hard.
You were meant for great things pretty girl.
Cheer up!

Missing

I let you aboard because I saw you
struggling out at sea.
I threw you a lifesaver and pulled you aboard.
I made you a fire and tended to your wounds.
Day after day, night after night,
you regained your strength.

I let you stay past your expiration
because you said you needed me.
But when we docked and parted ways,
the fog consuming my brain began to clear.
After days apart,
I realized that things were missing.

I walked past a picture of a person that
resembled me and realized that my smile
was gone.
Upon deeper observation,
I realized much more was gone.
Mama warned me that if you let the wrong
people in things like your joy, peace, and love
may come up missing.

LIGHTHOUSE

Inhale Courage, Exhale Doubt

I knew my life depended on it.
So, without hesitation I inhaled
the splendid beauty of courage.
Letting her take root on the freshly
tilled ground of my thoughts.

I inhaled slow enough to shine light
into the dark corners, and to olly olly oxen
free all unwanted hiders.
When my chest was filled I exhaled
and let go of all the violence of doubt.
Ridding myself of seeds, roots,
and all that could be poisonous to me.

LAKEYA BROWN

Inevitability of Brokenness

Brokenness is inevitable.
In our brokenness, we lose pieces.
They become lodged in places they
were never meant to flow into.
They travel to the heart,
they travel to the soul,
they travel even to major arteries,
disrupting the true order of things.

While trying to be whole again,
the broken pieces must be drawn out.
It hurt when it broke,
and it's going to hurt when it passes.
But it will hurt worse if they remain,
it may even cause contagion.
Don't despise the brokenness, it gives way
for the beauty of the light to bend.
It exposes each dark corner labeled as ugly,
causing it to exquisitely glow.

What a Shame

What a shame that many of us waste
day after day, year after year,
not growing, and never truly evolving.
We stubbornly refuse to live up to our
greatest potential.

Instead, we hide behind our neat
little lives, shunning the chaos of growth.
Not realizing we've outgrown it,
and having no one to tell us we
are giants in a dwarf's land.

LAKEYA BROWN

Wild and Free

I want to swim in the air that is wild and free.
I want to drink in the air
that knows no bounds only boundaries.
I want to be intoxicated
by its purity, overawed
and overflowing beyond that which is me.

Bare

The storm is often feared
because of its ability to expose.
The winds pick up
and you can't trace its direction.
There is no certainty, only the knowledge
that it is sure to leave you vulnerable.
No trees to hide behind or branches to hold
onto, just open sea and open sky.

There is no cover to take shelter.
Only waters that lay bare, threatening to wash
away the layers of masks
you've collected over the years.
The storm is feared because in one minute all
you have spent years trying to cover could be
washed away, leaving you bare,
and they may not accept
this true version of you.

LAKEYA BROWN

Extra Pieces

I need those pieces I cried to God.
No, he whispered.
In your becoming, on this journey
to greatness, I have completed you.
I need them, I whined.
No, he said again.
So I went behind his back and picked
out the pieces I thought would best suit me.
They fit perfectly for a while,
but then I became infected.
The infection spread, with no cure in sight.
Take these pieces away, I pleaded.
I don't need them! I don't want them!
Help me!
Without rubbing my mistakes in my face,
without hesitation, he took the attachments
That I had picked up, away.
I can't say it didn't hurt,
I can't say he didn't warn me.
Infecting myself, was my lesson in the end.

LIGHTHOUSE

What is For Me

What is for me will always be for me.
That is why I can relax.
I don't have to compete, seek validation, or
beat others down to make it to the finish line.

What is for me will always be for me.
I don't have to worry that it has passed me by
because only my fingerprint, only my attitude,
only my humility and gratitude
can unlock what is for me.

Lies We Tell

Sometimes we tell ourselves lies.
We ask, "What pain"?
We tell ourselves there is no pain, only bliss.
We feel it, but tell ourselves to bypass
it and not deal with it today.

One day turns into two days, followed closely
by weeks and months.
So we pack the exposed wound with human
connections, good or bad.
We use bodies to serve as illusions of warmth,
so that we won't be alone.

Anyone and anything to numb and silence
pain's screaming voice.
The voice beckoning us to pay attention to it.
Don't make pain an enemy,
choose friendship.
Pain will save your life
if you acknowledge its presence.

Decision

Making a decision is hard.
This is when your free will is tested.
To make a decision means to make a choice
and forsake everything else.

When making your decision
it is essential that you understand,
no decision is a decision.

LAKEYA BROWN

Heart Failure

When disappointment fills your core,
heart failure is near.
It lurks, crouching at the doors of
our heart ready to attack.
The choice is yours.

Feed your heart disappointment
or failure and it will betray you.
Feed it all that is good, lovely and pure,
and it will serve you.

People Want to Know Me

People want to know me.
But they don't want to KNOW me.
Few people want the parts of me that
are cold, wet, and unsanitized from
years of still water.

They only want the parts that produce enough
clean water to quench their thirst.
Once they have had their fill,
they won't think twice about me.
Not until they thirst again.

Unsure

It's not that I don't want to swim.
It's just, so many people have used
me as a life raft to save themselves.
Now I'm unsure about you.

I know it's not fair to you but this
is where I am.
Staying ashore would be better than
the agonizing thought that you
would use me too.

Forgery

I showed him the forgery,
but he asked for the masterpiece
that was me.
I obliged and showed him my
bold, true colors.

I obliged and showed him the ugliness
and the rawness.
It didn't scare him away.
Instead, he accepted every aspect of me.

LAKEYA BROWN

I Knew It Was You

Because you made me see flowing rivers
where I once saw floods,
made me see steady foundation,
where I saw rubble and devastation.
Because you made me see sunshine,
where I only saw clouds,
I knew it was you.

I Felt You

I felt you.
There is a song that my heart
plays only when you're near.
I felt you.
One hand in my hand,
the other on my heart,
massaging it back to life.
It was as if you were saying
I'll help until it's strong enough
to beat on its own.
I felt you.

LAKEYA BROWN

Root Down and Grow

Everyone wants to grow.
Their innate desire is to rise
and bloom beautifully.
But how can one grow if they
refuse to root down?

LIGHTHOUSE

You May

You may lie to others,
but for your sake and
your sanity, be truthful to yourself.
Be truthful, be frank,
be unapologetic, be who you need.
Be what you need, be who you truly are.

I Know

Yes,
I know that it is dark,
I know that sleep depletes you
and you're more tired than before.
It is because your soul is tired.
I know that you're emotional
and your physical wells are dry,
But you can't stop here.
You are not allowed to give up.

Feed You

You're not always going to feel whole.
Pay attention to the parts of you,
that are hungry.
If one is not balanced, all will sound the alarm
that you are not well.

You're not always going to feel physically
strong, feed your body.
You're not always going to feel mentally
strong, feed your mind.
You're not always going to feel spiritually
strong, feed your spirit.

The heart is the most deceitful and savage,
that's why it is sentenced to life behind your
rib cage.

When it is starved like your mind, body,
and spirit it will devour lies in its quest for
nourishment.

LAKEYA BROWN

Light

When you have reached the end of yourself,
I will be there.
The light that you have ignored while in the
fog of your disillusionment.
The light you have repeatedly
sailed past for years.

LIGHTHOUSE

Sometimes

Sometimes during the process,
it seems like there is no progress.
Keep moving, it's the greatest trick
of the enemy.
Keep your goal in mind, pivot and adjust.
Don't throw it out when it fails.
Re-access and readjust the vision.
The vision gets stalled sometimes,
hit refresh and keep going.

Moving Forward

Sometimes it takes going back to move forward.
Not to stay, not to get stuck, or become complacent there, but so that you can be launched further into the deep.
Like an arrow launched from the mighty bow you are.
The past is necessary in order to be launched to meet your targeted destiny.
You must be drawn back in order to be released forward.

Imperfections Only

How affirming it is
when they say,
"Your imperfections
are welcome here,"
and mean it.

Exposed

Don't take it lightly that people
are willing to show you their scars,
wounds, and hidden places.
That's hard.
That's brave.
That's beauty.
That's vulnerability.
That is working to heal one's own self.
Let empathy guide you.
Let love rule you.

Beautiful Places

I have decided to take the unfamiliar
broken, dark paths.
It will surely lead me to beautiful places.
When you spend too much time in the
shallow end, treading water, and avoiding
the waves, you forget that the most beautiful
destinations require you to swim in the
deepest of waters.

LAKEYA BROWN

Darkness You Don't Scare Me

The darkness does not scare me.
I do not mind walking down into its abyss.
I will endure the fierceness of its wrath
and curl my back against its sharp edges.
I will endure it all if it means learning the
lesson for my sake, and the sake of helping
someone else survive.

LIGHTHOUSE

Be Strong Be courageous

The storm announced itself before the rain.
It teased me before the thunder
and cackled before the lightening.

My heart sped,
and the inner me said, I am afraid.
"Be strong and courageous"
a soft voice said.

Perfect love casts out fear
I repeated in my head.
I am strong and I am courageous,
I repeated until my heart steadied
and peace consumed me.

Storms

Storms are made to reposition you,
and to take away your malnourished roots.
Sometimes those roots are too damaged
so the storm must uproot them.
You need a brand new start, in an
environment that will feed you what God
purposed for you.
Take root.
Allow yourself to be repositioned.
Embrace the unfamiliarity of change.

LIGHTHOUSE

Closer, Cleaner, Relief

As I sailed across the sea,
closer to the lighthouse,
I began to feel lighter.
As I got closer I climbed out of the boat,
unalarmed by the hungry sea at my knees.
I could breathe.

All of these years I never realized the weight
I bore, nor the toxicity of the air
that filled my lungs.
Not until the weight was released
and I had reached clean air.

Unpack

Come in and stay a while.
Take off your shoes and
unpack your bags.

If you are willing,
I will show you things
you've never seen before.

If you want I will teach you
things you've never dared
to learn on your own.

Man-Made Storms

God did not create this storm.
This is a storm crafted by
the works of your own hand.
Created by selfish-ambition, anger, greed,
and your thoughtless choices.
Now you seek shelter from the harsh rain.
Upset and cursing God, but let's be real this
storm was crafted by your hands.
You sowed it and now
the harvest is yours to reap.

LAKEYA BROWN

Rhythm

There is a rhythm to this life.
If you cannot hear it,
if you cannot feel it,
it may be because
you're offbeat.

Exit Wounds

Trauma to the body, trauma to the mind,
trauma to the spirit.
All of them can take a toll on you.
They will steal the very
splendor that makes you, you.
If you don't take care of yourself,
you will not realize that
you've taken the hits, until the
exit wound becomes visible.

LAKEYA BROWN

A Warriors Scar

Never trust a person without scars.
Scars signify that life tried to overcome
you, but you won.
Scars are a warrior's documented story.

Never trust a person without scars.
They don't understand the language of
the warrior and they won't understand what it
means to possess such an enchanting memoir.

Feel It

You will try to numb it.
Don't.
To feel it deeply,
to let it hurt, to let it burn
and overwhelm you
is the greatest way to learn
the lesson.

One After Another

One after another the storms raged non-stop.
Soaking my thin layer of clothing,
permeating my epidermis,
and watering my thirsty soul.

Two-way Mirror

There will be times when you stand in front of
people shouting for them to stop.
You will scream for them to turn around,
and beg for them to see you.

See me!
Feel me!
Understand me, you'll shout.

I am here behind this two-way mirror,
desperately waiting for your
acknowledgement.
But they won't see you,
they won't feel you and they
won't acknowledge you.

Does that mean you cease to exist?
The reality is no, though emotionally it may
feel like a yes.

The reflection that stares back from the mirror
holds all the acknowledgement you need.

No need to beg to be heard, beg to be seen, beg
to be acknowledged, beg to be loved,
or beg to be understood.

Look in your mirror and affirm yourself.
Tell yourself,
I am loved.
I am heard.
I am seen.
I am understood.

Joy

Joy bubbled up and flowed out
kissing my cheeks causing my
countenance to shine brighter
than I could've ever imagined.
As bright as mama's
face and daddy's smile
on the day I was born.

Blue Balloon

When I was little, I lost my balloon.
It floated up into the open sky
and never came back.
Unlike most children I did not cry.
I was not disappointed, curious maybe.

I stood alone for a second, wondering
if I would be as brave, and fearless.
Wondering if I would travel as high
and as far as that little blue balloon
with the pink string.

Keep Moving

Even when you are frozen and consumed with
hurt, it is important to keep going.
When the winds have shoved you face down
into the mud and the rain feels like
cat o' nines on your back, keep moving.
Whether you are whole or broken,
keep moving.
Even when you have to crawl on your knees,
it still counts, so keep going.
You are still physically putting one foot in
front of another.
Keep moving.

Tap Out

Look at it.
Look that storm in the eye.
Give it a wink.
Blow it a kiss.
Speak to it with authority!
Then run full speed ahead
towards it, and
wrestle it to the ground.
Pin it there, until it taps out.

Lost

Sometimes you get lost in life.
It's like you wake up and you're flying
around in the eye of the storm with no
recollection of how you got there.

You're spinning out of control.
Circling around and around covered
in rain and grime as the wreckage
holds you hostage mid-air.

Nothing is certain in that storm.
So you reach out and try to hold on.
You hold onto anything, to anyone
in hopes that you don't crash to your demise.

Each Step Back

Each step back,
is working for your good.
Each setup,
is working for your good.
Each frustration,
each tear, all for your good.

Nothing Left Behind

He withholds nothing.
God uses it all.
The storm, the sun,
the blessings, the curses,
the good, the bad, the ugly,
the peculiar and the broken.
God uses it all.
Even me, and I'm such a mess.

Relax

Relax, you're human.
God planned for your mistakes,
your disobedience and your fears.
You'll have to take the alternative
route now, but you'll arrive at
your destination.
Stop. Recover. Move forward.
Don't forget to relax and breathe,
you're human, and you're going to
make mistakes.
Keep going, you can't stop here.

Scrapes

When I was younger and I would come
home with scrapes and bruises from
climbing trees and running in the woods.
The antiseptic always burned.

My grandmother would say,
"Gal if it stings that means it's
working, now hold still."

I didn't understand her logic then,
but now it's clear as day.
I didn't get it until I had to let you
go and endure the pain that shot
a billion stings to my heart.

LAKEYA BROWN

Leave it Alone

Sometimes I have to
remind myself to stop
trying to fix things.
Some things deserve
to be broken for a while.

Boundaries

We all cross the line sometimes.
It could be because we draw them in the sand,
because we don't want them to be permanent,
and we don't want them to be evident.
It's only natural that the tide comes in with
seashells and water and washes that line away.
Set your boundaries and bold them.
This time don't draw them on the sand,
but bold them in your heart, your mind,
your body and spirit.
This time make them binding and lasting.

LAKEYA BROWN

I Heard You

When you tell me you're sorry and it does
not go back to the way it used to be.
It's not that I don't believe that you are sorry,
or that you are not worthy of my forgiveness.
No, it simply means that I believe you,
but I don't believe that you will keep
me safe emotionally.
I don't believe that you will not hurt me,
again, and throw me overboard into the
hungry sea.

LIGHTHOUSE

Lost Yourself

You lost yourself there.
You lost your peace and
nearly lost your mind.

You weren't yourself there.
Your heart fractured and broke
into a billion pieces.

You became infected, needed surgery,
and nearly flat-lined from despair.
So tell me why you would want to go back,
when you barely escaped the last time?

Direction

When the winds pick up you'll
be sucked back in.
You'll try your best, but you won't
be able to change the direction
that the storm carries you in.
The course has been set.
The only changeable thing will be
your attitude towards the storm.

Undeniable Earth

There are some days when I feel
one with nature.
Blades of grass tickle the bottom of my
feet, as I sit on that old cranky porch.

Thunder rolls and instantly
I am paralyzed unable to move,
unable to deny the beauty
of the tears of the earth
as they blend into my skin
like foundation, applied by brush.

LAKEYA BROWN

Thunderstorms

I love thunderstorms.
It lets me know that the
Earth has her sad days too.
That I don't always have to
put on a brave face and be who
they expect me to be.
When I see the muddy waters
traveling through the storm drains,
I smile and raise my glass to the
sky in solidarity.
I toast the Earth and say
cheers to us girl!
Today I'm letting my mascara run too!

Pen and Paper

And with all of my inward chaos,
I placed my pen to the paper
and immediately it all drained out.

LAKEYA BROWN

Not a Threat

When I let go of what I thought
was supposed to be, the waves were
no longer a threat.
It rocked me gently to sleep as the winds
hummed the sweetest lullaby.

Strong

The most vulnerable are often
the most guarded.
Sometimes the lover needs that
love reciprocated the most.

Sometimes the most put
together, shatters.
I think people forget that.

I think they forget that the
strong is susceptible to pain too.
That we are not machines or robots,
but humans too.
Rest.

It is alright to be tired,
you have fought like only warriors
have been trained to fight.
When you are weary, and overwhelmed,
learn to rest and not quit,
like true warriors do.

Living on Purpose

At some point in life,
when you decide to live on purpose,
you stop being afraid to fail and begin
to fear not ever achieving those dreams
you talked about as a child.

Your Soul Deserves

Your soul deserves not to be watered down.
It deserves not to be duplicated, not to
be edited, photoshopped, or repainted.
Your soul deserves to be its authentic self.
To be what it was created in eternity
and placed in time to be.

LAKEYA BROWN

My Tears

My tears are the evidence of my existence.
The pain, the heartaches, and the scars all
packaged into their own tear drops.
Each of them, representing a shout of triumph
as they cascade from my cheek
and water my soul.
Merging together, creating a rainbow above its
blooming botanical garden.
A reminder to keep going because it's all
working for my good.

A Story For All

We all create stories for our lives.
Encompassing a beginning, middle
and ending, dictated by our past,
present, and future experiences.

No matter how your story began,
regardless of what it currently
looks like, just know that you
control your future.

If you are weary on this journey,
and tired of carrying it all,
it is you who makes the decision
to let it all go and walk away.

Walk away from what was
never yours to pick up and carry.
Walk away from all that no longer
serves your purpose.

First Save Yourself

I've spent a great portion of my life
trying to save others.
Focusing on them and neglecting me.
Ignoring that somehow my boat sprung a leak
and the inside was filling with water, quicker
than I could scoop it out.
Until, half of my ship was submerged
and the other nose high
as if I were the Titanic.
Ultimately, teaching me to save myself,
and then save others.

Just Like That

Just like that, as I tossed and turned
awake loosening the grip of sleep,
I noticed that my eyelids
were no longer heavy.
They opened like butterflies after the
shedding of their cocoons.

They scanned the room like dragonflies scan
the fields for blades of grass.
Just like that, I woke up
and I didn't think of you.
I didn't care if you were here,
or there, near or far.
Only that I was no longer burdened
and my peace had returned.

LAKEYA BROWN

When to Begin

Don't begin when it's easy or when
you think you have it all together.
Don't change then.
Change begins when it's hard,
and when it will cost you the most.

You Created Me

Sometimes I have to remember you
created me and not the other way around.
When my eyes are heavy from straining to see
and allowing the cleansing tears to pass
through, I remember that I can rest my eyes.
You parted the red sea.
You closed the lion's mouth,
and you provided oil for the widow.

You numbered my hairs, you catch every tear,
carefully numbering them
and placing them in a bottle.
You even feed the sparrows
and surely, you love me the most.
Sometimes I have to remember you created me
and not the other way around.

If You Do

If you're going to do it, do it wholeheartedly.
If you're going to do it, do it as though you
were entertaining angels.

Do it even if you have to cry through it.
Do it even if you have to laugh through it.
Do it even if you have to agonize through it.
Do it even if you have to crawl through it.

Continue even when the blood, gravel,
and dirt from crawling, mixes with your
bold colors and deep darks.
When your glitter loses its sparkle, still do it.

LIGHTHOUSE

Shining

Do everything with elegance
and perseverance because even when the
hardship dulls you,
with a little water and with a little wiping
your magic will be unmasked.

With a little love,
it will always shine through.
Because whether it is masked
or unmasked the light is still the light.

The Act of Forgiveness

When it comes to the act of forgiveness
it will be life's greatest lesson.
Not a day that goes by, will you not
believe it to be life's cruelest joke.

The greatest forgiveness is forgiving yourself.
Forgive yourself now and later.
Forgive yourself over
and over and over again.
Forgive yourself until you have found the
beginning of your peace.

Simply Wait

Remain seated at your table and listen.
Simply wait.
While you wait learn to be quiet,
learn to be still.
Bask in the gift of solitude.
Don't compromise,
do not become emotional.
The order of things will unravel itself to you,
it will roll with ecstasy at your feet.

Empathy and Love

Let empathy be your guide when healing
and performing surgery on all unseen scars.
Let love be your light as you sail
through troubled waters.

Safe to Rest

He turned to me and said,
"It is safe for you to rest".
So, I did.

LAKEYA BROWN

Walking Along the Shore

When you have been ship wrecked in the past,
you begin to fear the ocean, as much as you
fear the storm.
Replaying almost being swallowed into its
abyss like your favorite song.

You walk along the shore not really sure if it's a
beauty or a monster.
Yet, you walk along the shore,
each time, dodging the tide.

Until finally the water reaches your toes
and licks them ever so gently.
You walk along until it kisses the back of your
knees.

Each time the water getting higher and higher
and your soul getting braver and braver.
Each wave singing, calling you in,
telling you to never limit yourself, outside or
within.

LIGHTHOUSE

The Sun

When the rain ceased,
I came up to the deck
and watched the sun shyly
peak its head around a
mountain of clouds.

The sunrise after a storm
is the most beautiful and
most memorable.

When it had acclimated itself,
I played underneath its warmth.
When it grew tired of sharing
all of its greatness, and could
no longer stay, I watched in awe
as it made its breathtaking exit.

Breathe

Suddenly,
the breathing that was once shallow,
stained, reluctant, and forced became
deep and purposeful.

LIGHTHOUSE

What We Fear

I thought what I feared was the rejection.
I thought that it would be the failure that
would break me.

When the time came, it was not the rejection.
When the time came, it was not the failure.
Instead, my greatest fear was what we all fear.

It is shedding the skin of mediocrity and
breaking the safety of its walls.
It is realizing that the cage is not really a cage.

How could it be that when the door has been
open all along.
What do we fear?

It is unleashing the greatness that we have
been tailored to live in.
Leaving our fantasies and acquainting
our true selves.

It is the fear of setting others free from the
illusion of being caged.
Realizing that there is no choice between inside
of the cage, or outside.

Because there is no cage,
only the fear of accountability and the light of
our true selves.

I Miss the Innocence of It All

I miss the innocence of it all.
When love was love and not
the possibility of life shattering
heartbreak, and soul aches.
The knitted fibers of my being,
yearns for the innocence of it all.

LAKEYA BROWN

How to Measure Relationships

Measure people not from your own heart,
but by the repetition of their behaviors,
consistency, and respect for your boundaries.

But First

Oh the places you will go
and the beautifully broken roads
you will travel.
Oh the people you will meet
and the hearts you will feed and heal.
But first, your lessons will make you strong.

LAKEYA BROWN

You Must Believe

Even when no one else believes,
you must believe.
You must invest in you.
Prove to yourself and only yourself
that you will always be worth it.

LIGHTHOUSE

Every Mistake

Every mistake I've made,
every mistake I continue to make,
God uses them as bricks to
build my today, my tomorrow,
and my forever more.

LAKEYA BROWN

Count the Cost

I've decided that anything that
will destroy, taint, steal, or alter my self-peace
is too expensive, and too bad of a risk.

Save Yourself

We look for people to save us
and that is not fair.
We become angry and call them inadequate,
but the truth is people can't save you.
Whether they say it out loud or not,
people don't want to save you.
That's too heavy a burden.
People are fighting to save themselves
and fighting to stay afloat.
Don't be unfair, let them save themselves
and you take responsibility and save yourself.

Tell Me How Many

How many storms were created in your life
because of the strength of your words?
Count them, label them,
and then cancel them.
Place them in a message bottle
and cast them into the sea.
Let them drift away into the open sea.
Return home and create words of beauty.
Fill your life with all that is nourishing.

You Had a Choice

You had a choice and you chose to hurt me
instead of providing the ingredients for me to
heal.
You made your choice,
now watch me make mine,
not out of vengeance, but out of love.
Love for myself,
love for my God,
and love for you.

Feed the Universe

Sometimes you breathe it all in.
You have no choice.
You breathe in the love and the hate,
the truth and the lies,
the beauty and the ugliness.
The breath is not your choice,
but you can choose what you exhale.
When you exhale, breathe life
and love back into the universe.

Thrive

You've been on autopilot too long.
Your mind, body, and emotions have taken
comfort in functioning below their abilities.
I know that auto-pilot keeps the pain at bay,
but it is not enough to just survive.
You will always survive because at the bare
minimum that is what we were created to do.
Choose to show up for yourself daily,
choose to be present in each moment.
Be kinder to yourself and enjoy your life.
Do yourself a favor and thrive.

Don't Listen

I'm glad I didn't listen.
When fear tried to control me
and that cunning voice said,
"You're a mistake,
no one wants you,
and you have no purpose".

I'm glad I didn't listen.
I'm glad I kept going.
When the paralysis of fear
came to overtake me,
I'm glad I kept going.
I'm glad I didn't listen,
I'm glad I didn't quit.

LIGHTHOUSE

That Night

That night the stars kissed
the infinite sky
and the moon blushed.

I slept deep and free as
the waves peacefully crashed
against the rocks and exploded.

The oceans sang the most alluring
lullaby and my blanket swaddled
me as if it was my first night on Earth.

No Regrets

If I had to go through it again,
I would do it with grace, with courage,
and a better attitude.
In the end, even with the tears,
even with the brokenness,
I can say it was all worth it.
The storm was worth it.

If It Must Be

If it must be that we are but a moment,
it is my wish to leave my words behind.
I hope they make you laugh
I hope they make you cry
I hope they make things clearer
I hope they make you wiser
I hope they make you stronger
I hope they heal you to the marrow
and center your soul.
I hope they shine brightest at night,
directing and teaching you to endure
life's necessary storms.

www.ingramcontent.com/pod-product-compliance
Lightning Source LLC
Chambersburg PA
CBHW030325080526
44584CB00012B/718